LandTrust

poems by
Katherine
Hagopian Berry

Published by NatureCulture LLC

www.nature-culture.net
www.writingtheland.org

ISBN: 978-1-7375740-0-2

Front & Back Covers:
Seven Tines by Martin Bridge and design by Martin Bridge
www.thebridgebrothers.com

Interior book design: Katherine Hagopian Berry
and Lis McLoughlin

Acknowledgments

"Before your shiva, a shark," *Tellus: Quaderni di Letteratura, Ecologia, Paesaggio.* Number 3, 2022 (forthcoming).

"Prayer for the Warblers," *Deep Water, Portland Press Herald.* August, 2022 (forthcoming).

"Mud Season," "Pitch Pine," "Trailblazer," "Thaw." *Writing the Land: Maine.* Forthcoming (NatureCulture, December 2022).

"Damariscotta Springtime," *Lincoln County News*, April 7, 2022.

"Sestina for Building," finalist, *Belfast Poetry Festival*, October 2021.

"Landtrust," "Before we reach the Skelton Dam," "Day before her birthday," "Dahl Wildlife Sanctuary." *Writing the Land: Northeast.* (Human Error Publishing, 2021).

Text for "Golden Shovel, Crucible" from *The Crucible* by Arthur Miller.

Text for "Day before her birthday, Dahl Wildlife Sanctuary," from a sign posted at Dahl Wildlife Sanctuary.

Table of Contents

From Here

Epilogue

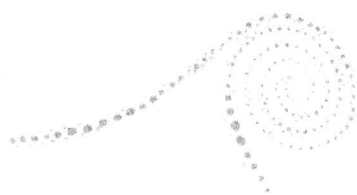

Adam, Sophia, and Chris, always
and for my father, builder

Landtrust

This is the magic
you walk the land
take nothing, not even your eyes
you must close them
until there is no looking
only darkness like an open hand.

This is the magic
place one foot in front of another
like a trail blazed on your bones
embrace wandering
some iron in the blood
leads you safehome.

This is the magic
the treasured knife,
the mica stone,
above you sky unrolls
a maryshawl of blue,
to hold them.

This is the magic
every lightray pressed
to your heart like a lover,
every newbud leaf,
like you, it will fall
like you, it will come back changed.

from Away

Vishap of the Armenian Mountains

My people built in circles
vishap, dragonstone, watervisa,
fishtales signal wellspring, danger
ramshorns spiral pasture, hope.

There should be true naming.
There should be a glossary of signs.
Woman mountain to tell me
with her red hands,

how to sanctify,
how to make this earth my own.

I know they buried them.
When they faded,
when direction failed,
in their falling, temples to the stones,

made vase, icon, shard, obsidian,
scatterfragment dark
like broken space, like jellyfish,
a swallowing

as if to return the stone to water
draw water from stone.

Remember how Vishap fell to earth,
made a path of his falling,
carving canals of freshwater,
cradling all the loss he found.

In the meadow, only blue
remaining, the course
of our lost wandering,
echoes like a broken stone.

Adam in Armenian

At the source of all the rivers
Adam spoke Armenian
firetongued phoenix, dur
our father flameborn
rising rubyred, singing
rubaiyats, a villa door
painted on a postcard
you send me with this book,
my language, I cannot
even speak or read. Yet

I know how the door
opens, patterns
of initiation knockknee,
childnaked, moonless
nights an ancient
history, we forsake
these whips of grain,
ears of corn, backturned veils
sibyl eyes still lumen
words some laughing god
mounted on your spine,
along the road of all
your bones, a snowbird
alphabet tracked in vision
language pilgrim, refugee,
exile, the book
on the desk in the quiet
room like a lamb
ready to eat
from your stilled hand.

The only word I know
is mayr, mater,

martyr, the faint

rose scent ghosting
cedar cabinets,
afternoon thunder,
black shawl, a plate
I eat from, mouthing
lost sounds, sacred
rootwords, a holy meal.

Postcard from the Bridgton Walgreens

I was born for migration
fly south each winter, dry arms
healing, side by side with yours.

This year all things must wait
Yesterday, a vernal swallow slammed
into my window, wild for flight,

while I, empty in the parking lot
rush the ravenous beak, glass door,
waiting area, baring the pale worm

of my arm, eager for needlebite,
one last reminder of cold.
Holidays on calendar pages

like redwings, like rubythroats,
like the roadmap
of a monarch's coastal margin,

All creatures know the way south,
toward some illusion of freedom
nest hallowed, empty, that gap

that comes in morning, ears stretched
for answer, rooster of my heart
crowing, some bright sunrise cry.

Russian Forces Surround Kiev

and the peace pole is missing from the church garden.
Remember, that brightyear, all our children in a circle
say in English, say in Chinese,
in Arabic, in Hebrew, in Russian,
let there be peace on the earth.

Now just a plastic bluebird in a fake nest
windchimes stagnant, lone appletree
in the garden barebranch,
everything biting its tongue
twisting like tactical maps,

land which has been claimed and reclaimed,
initials which transform themselves,
it could be your name, it could be mine,
it could be Eurus, eastwind, misfortune,
the one we don't talk about, so very broken,

I find the peace pole
in the corner of the parking lot,
white paint chipped by winter freeze,
imagining bombs, half-melted ground
I part dead earth,

tonguetips of crocus buds, greenhope, a protest
or just my footprint scarring the muddy garden
boottreads, tanktracks, armies advancing,
a shadow I can't help casting
on the waking ground.

Mud Season

We are waiting on the mountain.
Every day I test the path
down to our rushing stream and back
see if I can risk the hike, not falling.
Springmuck takes you down
if you let it, dangerous as deepice,
call you won't answer, letter
that stays on your desktop accusing,
words you can't separate
from all the tears this winter cried.

Outside my window, the mudflow
suckstep river in the shape of water
swirled like an endpaper
these delays are holy, I know this
but my heart is the sneaker
I won't put in the washer
scar of so much failure
dirtying the soul.

Instead of Washing Dishes,

we walk out, a pause in the rain,
springtime evening dry enough to travel
no animal, the vernal mud, wheelruts,
worn snow, long twilight of broken bottles
like a veil pulled back on wrinkled ditches,
shrouds of clouds heavy enough to block stars.

Back too quickly, I stand by the frying pan
stovetop light a setting sun, halffull glasses,
emptybowls, our mouths,
see how carefully I dry each knife
on the towel that says, homesweethome.

When its bad enough you hide the knives.
When its bad enough even the stove is a threat.
When its bad enough there is no dinner,
each hour swirling down the drainer,
spoiled succor, shelflife over, expired.

I watch you tease out from the catchbasket
each grain of rice, wilted leaf, onionskin,
keep our pipes clear, the springwater running,
flower in the center of the chipped plate
blue like Spica, which could be

a kernel of wheat, which could be
a messenger, angelwing
or just the centerline on which everything
balances, fingerweight of my hand
still choosing yours.

A troubling of goldfish

1.
You fall in love with feeder fish
ghetto of a temporary tank, absent everything
except a drabbing of gray stone.
The fish are what moves,
so much color cloudy water seethes with life
your favorite, the albino,
long and white like a surrender,
body outlier, one to watch out for
you say you love him best.

2.
Patient we try, say, alltherightthings
feeder fish don't make good pets
they need bigger tanks, more food,
there is no fourteen day guarantee,
but I see your heart longing
for the one we leave behind
misshapen head, tender body vulnerable,
the eyes of a thing that knows its place in line.

3.
All the beds are full.
It is the same for everyone everywhere
no doctors, diagnosis, room at the inn,
small safe corner to put your terror down.
On tiny hands, flashed like scales,
marks children carve upon themselves
if you could you would cross your heart
but children are always keepers,
bright crowns pulled back carefully,
so you can see their eyes.

4.

If you hadn't told me it would ruin our pond
I would have bought all the feeder fish in the tank
mottled orange, meltsnow white, dirty brown,
and let them go. Imagine
how we would have dived,
bodies growing long and fat and brown
from the kelp in the water
yellow lilies we canoe out to every year.
Instead I nurture our tank,
pillowsoft ferns, warming light, treasure chest,
one fish, at least, will never know want,
feed joyfully along safe densities of ground.

5.

I try not to think about the ones I leave behind,
writhe of hungry bodies
each one a forty gallon tank away from freedom
but there is never enough plastic flowers, omnivore food,
waterwheel bubblers, love to go round.

Before we reach the Skelton Dam

Above the curse line, in New Hampshire
the Saco is a different river, so mild
kayakers drift, their music, paddles
like white flags across bent knees.

On the margin of the cobble barren
I can imagine a different beginning
bark, brigantine, ketch, sloop, seeking
dawnshore, palms over open hearts.

Below my feet the stones
in the shallows are all the colors
of human hands, water brushes
them one along the other, ever gentling.

I wade in. Imagine curses
lifting, knives, falls, broken
bodies sated, blood enough
for blood, even my blond son.

Walking back the trail, caterpillars
are melting from every hemlock, pinetree,
seeking redemption, I imagine some bright genus
reconciliation unfolding like wings.

At the LLBean I ask them
browntail moth, they say, invasive
a menace, flamerash, poison, no mercy,
they destroy everything they touch.

The first time it stung me

Remembering the softness of cotton
is also to remember thorn,
old plantations on school field trips
bees bold in dead fields,
softness of soft thighs.

When Romans first discovered cotton
they assumed the plants bloomed fleece
miniature lambs penned in the bud
relishing shearing, longing to be separated
from the weight of their skin.

There was a way the south had of saying slavery
without saying pain
there was a way of saying
mothers brothers children
without making you think of your own.

They passed the cotton boll around
so we could separate fibre from bract
clouds yellowed at the root.
Rubbing the barb hard,
flesh of my finger

fresh with ache,
how I found the bee
and carried it carefully from my body,
woody stinger, brushed flank
the way it traveled down my skin like a lash.

You ask me to picture thirty years in the future

I cannot know what it is like to lose the land.
I have not lost my mother or my father,

I imagine their deaths like I imagine streams
some scorchdrought summer,

memory of water teartracing
on the facing stones.

I sit among them searching for something
not monument, not heavy with what once was.

Bathe in the water, take your feet to the river
whisper words of comfort, you know what comes next

long walk hillside, gilded dust, echoing the latesun setting,
all one glimmer, one root,

the bud which will eventually flower
one forest, one shade of green.

Pitch Pine

pyrophyte on Bald Pate Mountain
we say prune like it's easy
to let anything still living, go.

All of us hoarders,
seedcone days like childphotos stacked,
scaled and bract, impervious

until heat spreads us open like a palm,
Parkinson's, leukemia,
failing kidney, failing liver

cancer cells like fascicles
bright berry tumorous, the place
where once something better grew.

Twisted things can heal us if we let them
resintears sealing open sores
swollen muscles, soothing

even you, phone in your pocket
climb the mountain,
bandaged in silence,

find a view without any clear end,
thin hand on tan leg
this one gift I can give you

a day with nothing in it
empty like a granite ledge
negative margin, blank scan.

Saturday hike with ventilators

I took my children to the lake today
because you might be dying.
Everything moved more slowly,
as if you were there with me,
feet in the shallow, clear water,
lightspray of tanarms splashing,
suturing the sky.

Imagine, your seablue blanket
could be water,
just a summertaste of cold.
Imagine, the light
on your closed eyes
could be the sun.
Imagine, dragonfly
sipping at my shoulder
wings of your IV
tears like a tube in my throat
one hand on my chest
as if I can make it rise and fall
for you.

Paint dark trees against the sunset,
steady well-inked line
of a heart that keeps on beating,
death like a darkshell clam,
burrowing back beneath the sand,
no need to crack it open,
my heart knows you are the pearl,
scar the rapture, future nacre,
hope of more.

Imagine, your seablue blanket
could be water
just a summertaste of cold.

Imagine, the light
on your closed eyes,
could be the sun.
Imagine me
standing like a dragonfly
at your shoulder.
Imagine our laughing,
the bright road home.

Before your shiva, a shark

bald fisherman, bright hook
we flock like bait fish
see the sharp fin, see the dangle tooth
death like a kept promise
at the end of an invisible line.

It's just a baby, I say. An accident,
the fisherman, hands flopping, lowers
the shark back to breaking water.
I watch its tail drag across the sand
a pictograph, a rune.

It can't breathe, I say.
Red pulse of the gill
my own exhale,
a world without you,
raw in heart.

Bit by bit we cut it free,
my voice, pliers and beltknives
everything but the hook,
impossibly sharp
a whole jaw lost to pain.

Don't worry,
the fisherman says,
it will work its way out in time,
healing overtakes us
the ocean is half our blood,

I gentle the shark
as we finally cut it free
each brutal wave
each shudderbreath,

drags it back to shore.

I need it to live for you,
swim the unfathomable dark
with all the persistence life can muster.
I need it to find its mother,
some path beyond pain,

the shark and I, in silhouette,
one beach, one waning sandbar,
my hand reaching out
swings the shark wide
like a silver rainbow over the water,

no space between its wild motion
and my own, only what we have
in common, fight, this breath,
one sudden dive
and both are gone.

Hot Springs

At the hot spring
I see as if a stranger,
another southern railroad town
kudzuvine veiling, dead trees ghost

rapid fierce river, full in flower,
sweetbee nectaring,
mountain rising, all roads
rough from passing storm.

There is nothing to holy,
nothing to baptize, nothing to tell you
how my blood still keeps time
with the three am train,

waking in my sleeping bag,
like arms around me,
roar of the river, cavern water,
root uncurling, night moth circling,

like me it is drawn to fire, like me
it shakes death off its wings, lovehungry blur,
who can know which light it longs for,
which dark parting it calls home.

Kudzu

like madwomen, the maples
have worn a furrow in the power lines
we watch them in their bathrobes of vines
shuffle through days, sucked dry and bowed down.
Eventually the GPS fades, pulled over
in the bible church parking lot.
It's not as obvious as it seems;
we are not simply the trees;
we are the old van making it down one last hairpin turn,
we are the broken elastics on the shifter,
we are the church, problematic sanctuary;
we are mothers in the car slamming
palms against drained phones
secretly delighted no one can reach us
for days, we can be without metaphor
pull out a second juice box, find another
pillow we have made from our own arms
something soft enshrouding,
something green which banks,
lets these bright fires rest.

We linger at the campground exit

because to leave means winter,
means silence, but most of all distance,
folded-down tent, six foot boundary,
the way we can no longer hold or be held
stranger at your table, table set for one
morning like carcrash, like catastrophe,
lockdown, another wave.

We have sat quiet in our cages,
prayed for hope to heal.
We have put away distraction,
blue light, flickerscreen.
We have bathed in the water.
We have washed in the water.
We have drunk the water,
felt something knit back together,
a ghostbone of connection.
We have let the ground sing us to sleep,
hair curling, jasmine dripping,
sweeter than sweet from the stalk,
each night moth lingering
to taste and retaste.

Last orison of fawn
across the dewfield
unbelievable softness
of a latesummer morning
leap joyful, separate,
our departures, the new
day, its unignorable chill.

Persephone at Kea

On Kea, death is heat
splitstalk the grass,
scorched slit fraying
furrow dust, sun chariot
crazing dry fields.

Empty the vineyard,
withered the vine
even the oak seed, stripped
of its laurel crown
bleeds tannic into rock.

The path is too loose
to hold your footprint
remembering weeds,
Jerusalem sage soft, resilient
you wish it would draw blood

give you something to save
anything living to sketch
fingertips still trembling
at the memory of bee orchids
blooming solitary in the ditch,

at first you thought
the rich brown of their hearts would fly
as you raced to trace them,
dying pomegranate
each treasure hour, wilting

flower, newbud, nymphic,
hallowing cool morning
before dayheat drags
its scythe across the sky,
before the dark dawn comes.

Tips for Avoiding Bear Conflicts:
Remove & Store Inside

Bird Seed

broken feeder, cut waterbottle
drudged with silt and too much summer
rain on scragglepine, apple tree,
trash you say, roots unsound. Old
kitchentable stenciling a birdhouse
two colors in layers, brown
fur on darker brown, I am afraid
of bears, stay inside the lines,
you growl, sit quiet down.

Garbage

all over the garage, Lennox Eternal
clawfoot tables, darkwood memory
they say moving is easier with fewer
possessions, class pictures, polar
bears on colorpages, uneven
family trees, I can't remember
when the argument started, distance began,
my face, a shield, my smile or,
more honest, this mask.

Grills

on report cards, class schedules
even the car I crashed once
rearending a Kodiak, ignorant
of stops, my heart a hurricane
and you sat beside me in the bed
that swallowed my grandmother
quilting bare shoulders, blanketed
in so much handmedown pain
I no longer felt alone.

Livestock and Pet Food
one move too many, you, allergic,
gave my sister a cat, monsterbear,
pushaway, we just thought
you hated it, or even us,
long braids like keychains
we gifted you, constant
you carried them, until all
the shallow words of love
wore clean, left only gold.

The ivory-billed woodpecker was declared extinct today

which is why I threw a fit about paper napkins.
They called it the Ohmygod bird,
because when it used to unfurl,
black and red like a nationflag
people couldn't help themselves,
worshipping, down to knees or cameras or just
the blank film of their wideopen eyes.
My mother cannot resist family
sized bags of paper napkins, wrapped in plastic.
I used two tiny pieces of paper towel today,
they should have been rags. I know

my individual carbon footprint
did not kill the woodpecker, who needed
old growth, live oak, yellowpine,
poplar and chestnut, that flourish,
the south makes a habit of denying itself
forests, burial grounds, red throated bird
all sacrificed for progress, which looks like
expulsion, flaming sword, cindercross. I know

we are all dying out. Child in the hospital,
followup scan, unfinished math worksheet,
high cholesterol, antidepressants, funeral,
scars, four cavities, two arrests, unemployment,
happymeals, Medicaid, the forms all
start to look the same after a while, failure
every single line, a breath
you can never quite take. It's why

we are all heading to church today.
On the ground we will place
the whole year. A circle. We will say
there is no beginning, there is no end.
We will touch the block for Pentecost, red

like the crown of the woodpecker
we will touch the ivory star, mated voices,
waiting on rebirth. We will tie each thread
together, gold like talons, our fingers
hold on, blessing, reblessing
the days we have left.

If we are all God's poems

how can the lesson for today
be the Ark and the Tabernacle
God of Law, unnamable
who knows a thing and keeps it holy
who erases nuance,
lays out the sacred plan?

Still, there are two arks, one
for rules, one to resist them,
to save what can be saved.
There are two tents, one
to make a gesture of permanence
one born from remainder, the discarded

is what I bring, not holiest of holies
not sacred, not priest,
not cloth of gold,
not cherubim, wheels or wings
not incense or candle or laver or alter
not bloodred leather, not even the ram.

Just what you gather when you walk out
behind the church on a November evening,
raw sun sinking low on the beeches,
vivid orange, rosepurple, gleaming
before it all ages brown, dropped branches
smooth on your hand, sap pungent like smoke.

Above you the sky is an ocean,
crow could be raven, hope its harsh cry.
Like nest, I build the tabernacle
twig by twig, roofed in what I find,
enough to keep dry, enough to warm hands,
together in shelter, we are all the dove,

enough eyes gleaming
to make angels
of our own observing
the moon hanging huge
like a question,
the embering fire.

Saw-Whet Owl found in Rockefeller Center Christmas Tree

Uprooted, the universe upended
and you, small and easily camouflaged
along for the ride, some ironsky morning
needlebare, your sunburst eyes, exposed.
So they find a box to fit you in,
blanket all the familiar allrights,
free you, released, rehomed
one forest enough like another
but everything horrible with difference
the sun in the wrong place in the wrong
bowl of the wrong color sky
and where is the mountain? Where the voice
that used to answer you? Where the familiar meal?
Your wet cry like something torn apart
all rough edges and hope for a future
and yet, I wonder, how much longer
can you last?

Persephone Puts Up Her Christmas Tree

It is hard to be thankful with so much want.

Hell has too many rivers, each one a temptation:
end it shallow, wade deep with stones
give up daybyday, one foot
another, brushhair, getdressed,
set tables enough they can feast without you.

Hell has too many caves,
each one ripe for collapse
shutdoor, breaklamp, sealcrack
until smotherbreath wraps you like a blanket,
the rough scrape of hands can end.

Hell has too many monsters, each one hungry
for eyes to pluck out, livers to gnaw upon,
stone so heavy on my chest even fruitless
pushing takes power, lie down, the warmsoft ground
slowly sinking, my own grave.

Why not decorate early, so the whole cave shines
beat plastic branches, eat electric fruit,
every papier-mâché angel with the year
and your name, childfaces that remind me
of my mother, pinkcheek, soft wind, pomegranate spring.

Trojan Asteroid 1172, Aeneas

So this is where you end,
trailing Jupiter, rockarmored Achilles,
the Greeks, Priam and Hector,
so far across the solar system
I cannot see you with the naked eye.
Just another lost Roman, weeping
tears of gas and ice, luring camera lens.
Even heaven has a place for transformation,
across the blank expanse, a glimpse
your first wife or second, sons,
a daughter, the woman
who haunts you, 209 Dido,
so much closer to the sun,
it might be a different universe altogether.
She has gone
to join the charioteer, Auriga,
vowing never to be caught again.
Entombed in the magnetdust
of distant orbit, left
to ponder universal absence,
hands I once touched,
your body, rotating even now,
in its shroud of stars.

Prayer for the warblers, dead on my houselot

gold necks stretched cold,
rigor mortis, everything frozen,
even the candleflame
drowning in its bathtub of wax.
It was an omen, you say,
drugs, isolation, two lost birds
together in a fresh budding tree
pulsebeats, their brokewings
dapple to dapple until cold
snapped, dawnsong, trillalarm, call
your hand on the phone, seeking
some high nest, the thinnest freest bow.
You say every candle can channel
spirits inflamed, wait for it to flower
even in glass jars, even this old prayer
say heaven, say, home of many wings.

Burning our palms

Giving it to fire won't make it better.
Leaves ash, like flame,
curling margins,
that mourn in the blood.

How your heart beats one name,
and then another,
and then the thing
you cannot name.

This is not why we come to fire.
This is not why we rend.
Not why we douse the candles ourselves
walk mudtrails, sacrifice, the ruts in our roads.

Nothing of grieving is ever over.
The life in the stalk lives
in the ash lives
in the bodies of burned stars. Lives.

Its why when everything is stirring underground,
spring, that warm exhale,
we trace ash like a scar for everyone, visible,
what it took this time around,

The wound in the palm
invites you, as I invite you:
Press a finger in.
See how my pain beats beside yours.

Enough of misery to symphony
soft weep, flash flame,
the fire now red, now blue
the breath now in, now out,

The way we watch silent
feel heat in the ground after
everything else has faded
into obvious calm, a few flakes of snow,

but we know it seethes,
still immortal,
the center of the earth
still boiling, still bone.

from Here

Avalon Perigee

Sister, I come to you
across the hard mountain
shards of our forgetting
mosaic in my hands.

Wild song pinons
the dark dreamroad
shares the oneeye,
mineral vision magnified

like light in water, water takes time,
time takes us, malleable air,
lake mist rising, always flowering
perigee, the waiting moon.

Outside in the driveway,
my daughter and I grounding,
pressfeet trembling
into granite, obsidian, chipped mica

crystalline, a heart-cry
as if sound could make a road
wide as moonlight ribboning the stillake
wide as a mother side by side with a daughter

wide as history, and I
could stand beside you
as shadows stand
the scars that shroud the moon.

ABCs of New Construction

Architects are expensive, so we use the
basic plan, beginner blueprints: Northwoods
Cabin, 28 by 32, our
development devoted to natural succession,
easements for beaverpond, vernal stream, tanglewood, one
field, remnant, miles distant up the mountain.
Given, there will always be delays.
How can anything be built to last
if you don't make space flexible
joist forgiveness, acceptance,
know the pause of falling rain.
Later, so much will be covered over,
memory our lathe, the surface crack, the bent
nail, error just a reminder to
orient hope, a new house always
possibility manifest, until, February deepfreeze, our framer
quits, leaves only bones, the
rafterribs gaping, we lose heart.
Snow collects on lumber piles like a shroud. Setbacks, I
understand them in
theory, but patience is a virtue I
usually lack. I must release these
vacant dreams like
weepholes, our house once
xenolith, now I notice, bluesky has roofed us
yawing rafters gray sisters to the birches, all
zoomimic, we cannot see the house for trees.

You told me the red winter squirrel

could be my animal
and I ignored you, imagining
whales soft with oceans, imagining
moose antler-heavy, lilied breath
my mountain pond.
Surely my body must announce itself,
stop and take notice, pull over photograph
the largest thing in the room.
But you may have been right,
gutflat for shelter
all the world hoard,
thousands of small piles piledup for later
buy the bandaids, I tell you,
we are running low, all the rainbow
masks, pants one size too big
the next gift, and again the next.

Winter is my preoccupation,
anything that can kill you
when you aren't really looking,
They say death by freezing is comfortable,
snow your blanket, ice a mobile,
refracted light fractures
into prismacolor, they say
even trees will lullabye
that close to the end,
all except the squirrel
shadow-tailed, bow of its body,
bridge between worlds, it will
spit its life upon you
claw until it clenches
your heart pulled back to savor
this hunger, and survive.

One potential origin of baklava

is the ancient Roman dessert, placenta
extinct succor, just like the maples, forfeit for progress,
millionaire condos overshadowing kitchen windows,
bricks still warm behind the gas stove.
You wave empty cups like protest flags
coffee thickening on the burner, in the small brass pot,
briki, like my great-grandmother's,
longing for bitter, sugar, *metrios*,
we all say together
even though this is not quite the language
I remember from my childhood speaking.

The counter is the same, though,
broad and flat to roll sheets of philo
cutting down an extra paintbrush
to spread butter, honey, memory
of my great-grandmother's arms
like waves as they crossed the dough,
glazed, folded, the green nuts waiting.
Baklava is easy when made together
mother, aunt, daughter at the counter
aging, diamond subtle, still on our tongues,
sweet names linger, the ones we have lost.

Nocturne with my daughter's nightmares

Tonight before you have bad dreams
let us take off our bodies together
leave them on the floor with amputated socks
t-shirt cadavers, sightless lenses of our glass eyes.
Now only white bones that shine in moonlight
let these skeletons, too, dismember.
Remember when we were both only atom
you inside me, inside everything dark?
Unlearn your words for terror, danger,
make wild the sounds of old fears,
put on scales, softfur, wings
sharpen every baby tooth.
Beyond the narrow window, we
are nothing but nightmare,
peeper frogs, their arias
sonarbats, the spiral wind.

On the way to confirmation

the car in front of us has
the license plate, THY WILL
Sometimes omens are obvious,
backs of Audis, insides of fortune cookies,
sometimes just the shadow
of a wing on the ground,
hawk resting outside my window,
buck I surprise solitary on my evening walk
sunset, his flank, the twilight moon.

Inside, there will be incense and music
There will be a laying on of hands
Someone will say spirit,
someone will say separate
false things from true.
There will be you, in your newcreased pants
fighting for stillness on the narrow pew,
there will be that moment in the car,
your face crumbled in anger and its aftermath

I'm trying to talk to God,
you say,
but I don't know how.

Everyone has left the church
and it's just us and the empty parking lot,
white cross of snow on the blacktop,
starstitched robe of winter sky.
Up the empty isle together,
your fingers still so small in mine,
behind the altar, lost star, a wild satellite
stubbornly orbiting, and,

just like that,
holy.

You say, God so close.
God so close,
the olivewood cross
(color of sand, of bread, of ground)
from the cloth bag they give me
(color of rust, of earth, of blood)
the chalice of our palms.

Thanksgiving

I smooth my favorite tablecloth,
tallying the stains, serve grapeleaves
rolled with rice, a paradox

oilysmooth, lemontart, crisp
stone mountains wrapped in viridescent fields
breeze leavened, the hot summer days

How once, even my mother canned
rich earth of her own garden
How once, there were blueberries wild on Federal Hill,

my father picked them as a child,
tasted morning on the backporch
brightknit like an afghan

so I make you write your favorite memory
on construction paper leaves.
You say real plants have rough edges.

I say there is nothing wrong with omission,
how all this becomes history,
kneewoven under wobbly tables

nails resting on scratched chairs
like small winter moons.
I want to age that way

rich with oil, wrapped in brighter memory,
bright leaf bursting open
nourishing the tarnished spoon.

Pietree Orchard

At the edge of the orchard
valleys are throwing their heads back
exhale fog into clearing sky,
ending gilding every apple
bold on its branch
last bee clinging joyous
to the side of the cup,

I take the lid off,
watch it sip and slip away,
even frostground longs
for the source of its lost fire,
hive strong for winter, air
scented apple overripe,
all the sundered fruit plowed back.
I hold the leaf my son gathered
in the palm of my hand, fight
not to put it back, exactly where it grew,
on the broad branch.

You tell me a nor'easter is brewing.
Between us, we have made
a warning of the world.
That night we let our children curl
like dry petals in the same bed
Fresh-pressed, our hands
enough to worship, mountains
bluing the distance, ridges
of your gentle palm.

When I wake, my mouth holds
the juice of your name.

The ghost in the church elevator was happy to see me

This is not metaphor.
New Englanders hallow their ghosts
like old addresses, exboyfriends,
lost diamonds, burned down farms.

The community life committee
agreed it was a little girl
who died before her time,
the parents, ghosts themselves,
built a children's chapel
and she must have tagged along
unable to leave them desolate
in the sparerooms of loss.
No one could pin down
how she felt about it, except
at some point, the adjacent elevator
must have proved more interesting than
white pews, sad carpet, reverence,
a matter of energy, or just self-expression,
finally making a sound.

Stick around long enough
and doors opening and closing
just seem like conversation.
You take the stairs.
Set an extra place at table,
chair in the children's circle,
leave out an empty pageant costume,
make room.

When I left, she was on my mind.
Take care of the ghost, I said,
not in a don't-cross-the-streams kind of way
but leave her flowers, bowls of milk,
tell her once in a while she

can elevator up beyond the peeling steeple,
past all our names, to what's next.

I don't say this easily.
You are the first people I've told,
and even then I've changed names,
lied to a reporter or two, some ghosthunters
nothing to see here. Move on.
And six years, pandemic,
everywhere silence,
I thought she had.

Until I came back,
my children learning French vocabulary
repeating one after the other
words for hello, for welcome,
for how have you been,
my dear lost friend
and I heard the elevator
restart itself, rumble
like a cat along my backbone,
miraculous ordinary,
Monday wondrous,
such cosmic gentleness
how time must look different to a ghost.

I want to tell her there's a school here now.
French in the parlor, cooking in the kitchen,
my daughter's old Christmas dress
still the angel costume,
I put it back on the shelf
make room for memory
like a ghost in my hands.

Things my mother saved

1/3 of a can of tomato sauce. Back of the fridge, congealed like cramped muscle, pulsing on my hands as I feed it down the sink, like murder, like failure to thrive, placental, like so much else we missed.

1/2 of a can of black olives. When left too long, olives spot with white, black branches after hard frost, tips of things exposed and shoved carefully back.

3/4 of a red onion. Digestion being what it is, you have to parcel out savor, palateshock, a mountain we wait to climb until my father's knee heals, plantar fasciitis fades.

2 shoeboxes of Christmas ornaments. My son loves them best, white cat with sparkles, small scratched toy soldiers all missing gilt. I remember quietly rubbing their plastic faces. I remember when the sequins fell. You sewed them back on and never told.

8 table settings. Don't put it in the dishwasher, you say, true gold will melt in heat, worthless. More precious, Autumn Wheat, free from Almacs, I remember thin paper books in marquetry boxes, green stamps like seeds, their growing weight, fassoulia, too bright for other tables, drops that fell on my plate like blood. My great-grandmother saying, let them, refusing to rub off the stain.

1 friend, crashgasp collapsed you found her on the travertine tile, a sudden huddle, almost gone, salvation, ambulance, blue and white patterns and fresh painted doors. Thankgod, you say, we checked, a moment of breath, panic that one day I won't do as well, be as close, make it in time.

Me, mostly. Psychologists weren't really a thing in the eighties, so I told the stuffed beaver puppet, hairy oldman hand, that school was easy, skipping a grade would be fine. No one asked about anger, or how many times I imagined dying, or even just that sense of leaving my body like a knife in someone else's hands. Who knows how messed up I actually was. Back then you could kick at stones for hours, push over trees, no one would stop you. You could ride your bike faster and faster and faster with no hands and all they would say is brave. Show me again. Until I fell, bleeding. It was my mother I ran to. Her hands that made me feel my own.

Trailblazer

There are many ways up the mountain.
Novice hikers should consider the orange loop,
a gentle meander, hawks, birches, even wood ducks
but husband and daughter, eager sneakers shining blazes,
ready muscles stacked like cairns
say they'll take the harder trail. My father

> still deciding, tight patentleather shoes, my father's
> eyes meet mine and part ways. Mountains
> don't judge. Dollars stacked in your wallet like cairns
> or emptyhanded happiness, the wild loop
> of zero, nothing left to lose. A voice that blazes
> past us, he's for Pate Trail. Elder Ducks

honk frenzied warnings, smiling, my mother ducks
her head around a chill of fear. "Your father
can't even see the blazes
these hazards, old men shouldn't climb mountains."
Too late to call him back, our path loops
over a gentle rise, at the next cairn

> we add a stone, like you do for a grave. Cairns
> when used for direction are called ducks
> across the balding headland they loop
> like the proud nose of a stubborn father
> what the mountain
> is already showing you, at the end blazes

are unnecessary, only maples blazoning
endings like fruit on the altar of the cairn
like waves of color on the mountain
iridescent cries of mallard ducks
and my father
out of sight on the hardest loop

of the most challenging hike. Just the narrow loop
of our voices to remind him, follow blue blazes
keep pace, don't rush, but my father
summits before all the others, we find him monument, a cairn.
Calmly he points the beak of the duck
true north, writes in his journal, Bald Pate Mountain.

You climbed a mountain, says the cairn.
Autumn blazes as it cools, weep the ducks.
Descending together, I loop arms with my father.

Tips for Avoiding Bear Conflicts:
Secure & Clean

Bird Seed
weeks before your visit my children
embrace creation, streamers
and cards, paperplate flowers, broken
birdhouse they pass back
and forth, carefully avoiding
collapse. Under oak trees, banners of color
I gather sticks from our driveway,
return to pattern stones hard as animal eyes,
the wild margin of our yard.

Garbage
fills up the woodshed
full plates, salty enough to sate memory,
another year locked away,
like the parquet box where
you have hoarded photographs
first my face, then my children's faces
haloed in the belly of the same painted bear.
You send another copy, unable
to refuse what we already have.

Grills
you say replace it, but I love
our grill bent from lobster
pot, firepit, caked with leavings
of so much feast, your body
beside mine handsteady
on dial heat, bearing tongs,
you still know when everything
is ready, you still know the perfect time
to turn it all around.

Livestock and Pet Food

I say goodbye with maple syrup
pictures I can't stop taking
autumn makes me think last and always last.
Father, we are getting older, moving
closer, I point to stars overhead,
cryptid names you taught me, restless
monsters, ursa major, leonid centaur
always chasing, always visible, this spiral
a mobius, our eternal return.

The day you told me you were pregnant

Our neighbors saw a bear,
furrumpled, waterseeking,
pulled toward something
larger than its own hunger—
The mountain, named for love.
Our lake, source of its own motion.

We give you dried summer flowers.
We give you all the gentle hands.
We say, yesterday we bought a boat for our son
and he spent an hour tied to the back of his father's kayak
blue trailing blue, like damselflies
rescuing each other from the water.

It took me jumping in.
It took me standing beside him
kneedrenched and splashing,
before he slipped the knot,
dipped his paddle like a wide white paw,
our cove another set of arms.

We are all desperate to safen the world.
We are all watching out for one another,
babycub at the birdfeeder,
track the wood with ready eyes,
until her shadow merges, sidebyside
and shielding yours.

We cannot labor with you, so I write this poem

You still in labor and my daughter
discovers a Minecraft labyrinth.
She plays for hours.
Follow the blue wall, follow the red
each contraction simulation
but still we walk it with you
amazed at our avatars,
familiar creature at the center
horned as if a reminder
that discovery is danger,
passion can injure, love
a clue slender enough to grasp in two fingers
solid enough to lead us back to light.

I wish someone would ask me how it felt
and want to hear the real answer,
how masks unmask leaving only your strength
how jeweled horns shatter
freed bones splinter
warm mouth shelters
at the end you are monster and mother
together, feet kicking out
wild with dark hair
eyes purpled in wonder
the pain of letting go
the thing you love most.

Socially Distant Family Picnic

Clam chowder grit with seasalt
on deserted beaches gray
with thunder, distant

picnic on old towels, we notice
someone has made a driftwood
monument, neaptide waxing

braiding dulse and old trapwire,
skeletons of seaborn salmon
knock the air like chimes.

Like riptide, like undertow,
pulled to add our scavanged
treasure, topazblue cord

I tie around sea lettuce spread
like a fan on drying sand
broken crab you find

at the wateredge, past deepholes
and spinning lures, wavestamped
beach and maretailed cloud

gathering gentle death
this brutal meat, this claw
shell strewn strata

I can brush away, easy
as a palm on your small foot,
as clouds sweep out to sea, these storms.

The day you get your braces on

[red deer bracket the highway * we pause wirebound * I think of all we are trying not to break * Queen Anne's lace popcorning the shoulder * caramel haunch of the deer * endless line of summer cars frantically cautioning * honk like migrant geese * It all gets lost so quickly * Nervous in the dentist chair * blue flicker of lake outside the window * tiger lilies beating on the sliding glass door * all the dos and donotdos * all the cards of rotting teeth * all the deft maneuvers * first limit for your feast * I know you will follow the rules * choose elastics beachrose pink * baby blue * creased lips * in my hand * the vanished flank * jagged nacre of your last tooth * enamel faded * rust-blood remnant * my body wild * still welling at the root].

Red deer, we pause, think
It all gets lost, vanished flank
your blood, my wild root

My son is obsessed with the Battle of Midway

where Dauntless bombers dive like seabirds
on the boats in the water. What
were their names, daddy
what lever, which rod, how
did each explosive skyegg fledge
flashed from its aluminum nest?

I race to translate the names of carriers
carcassed, cindering the whitecap
Redcastle, Increasedjoy,
Greendragon, Dragonflight
gallery of my body rising over this blue
deskchair, a space for you to lapsettle, land.

When a boat sinks, there is a hole
the size of its leaving in the water,
it will suck you down, a whirlpool
of your own making. I want you to remember
gentle departures. I want you to remember
the knot in my heart that is yours.

Golden Shovel, Crucible

Not real, my daughter says, *a*
fairywing impractical to carry coin, crystal, a *child's*
droptooth, and, anyway, who would welcome a *spirit*
ravenous for bone? Doubtless doubt *is*
necessary, some things will eat you alive, *like*
gutfear, loss of control, *a*
weight I carried long before I bore you *child*.
I try to tell *you*
some things are worth unproving. I *can never*
imagine life without the throat*catch*
of magic on the moon, darkwood wonderglimmer. *It*
is hope that roots us, you should know *by*
now, impossible things are the ones worth *running*
toward, hard, until you fall *after*
them into story, find dragons, ride them if you can. *It*
is nature's impossible bumbling, it is *you,*
the wonder of the world. We *must*
find a place to *stand*
dilemmahorns just an opengate, *still*
believing in our lost belief, *and*
hope

for love, it will soon itself come back.

Damariscotta Springtime

I know I should be singing,

Dawnland is waking, thicket barren, coiled fiddlehead,
pinebough denning, brownbear pawing,
all of it listening, demanding I step:

empty chapel, half-melted candle,
remember how we blessed it, shoulder to shoulder,
bright belt, our bare feet, circling time?

Behind us the sun rose when we asked it to
the moon came to save us from loneliness

and I, like streambed, like fullegg, warmfeather
nesting, burrowing deep, perfect in fractile, all this web,
singing where once water sang.

It works in me, longing,
looncry, frostnight, danger and wonder
like red embers burning, the sounding,

our voices, the bright bringing dawn.

Day before her birthday;
Dahl Wildlife Sanctuary

On the silver maple trail, *we*
wonder have we seen it all, *realize*
we have forgotten the rare cobble barren, *that*
longed for habitat, hairy hudsonia, silverling, *vegetation*
dragonnamed, but the sky isn't *clearing*
stray raindrops, open shoes, all untied, it *is*
easier to circle, *a*
fragile spider, half orbiting *messy*
nest box poles, barbed wire, *transition*
meadow, the falsenettle, mayflower, bellwort *and*
you are almost twelve, taking selfies, *visually*
flinching, worry contorting your eyes, are they *unattractive*
your legs like a fiddlehead poised to unfurl? So *we*
learn to notice the gold in our hair, cease to *apologize for*
nearsight, the way it forces attention, *the*
truth is our whole *short-term*
preoccupation with *appearance*
is nonsense anyway, I tell you, *we*
are alone in the field, there *are*
creatures in stickdens huddling close, *glad*
of their dark bodies. I have saved only one picture, *you*
like a raptor, listening for water, *have chosen*
profile, birchbark, floodplain, thicket *to*
remember our *visit*
capture the cloudsky, the swale, the meander scar, *us.*

Sestina for building

In the garage we are sealing pine
paneling, yellow
dog sleeping, new birds
rocking egg, they will not break
or fly. I think about motion as I spread the stain
back and forth, steady pace,

arc, return, brush again, so often the pace
of living snares me, pining
for something permanent, memory stained
like the yellow
throat of the warbler, wings breaking
under ice, the freeze, we brought the birds

inside, frantic, warmed each bird
with our urgent breath, the steady pace
of progress breaking
like ice from the roof, pine
plank wet with rain, then yellow
pollen from birthing bud, staining

everything, beginning again, and I am straining
to hold it all together, bird
untucking yellow
wings, hammer pace
strength of pine
every splinter break

I want to sand it down, break
each flaw open, if stain
runs out I will use blood. Pine
knots look like guardian angels, godbirds
of prey to outpace
my fears, yellow

beaks to stab them. I rub the yellow
board bone, a spell of protection. I break
these bonds, pace
sand and stain
and hang to dry. The birds
fly the nest. I see them in the white pine

shaking shells off their wings, I match my pace
to their first flight, yellow birds, black pine
break dawn, stain the ground with sky.

Psalm 23

The Lord is my shepherd
I shall not want
He makes me lie down
in green pastures
He restores my soul
He leads me in right paths
for his name's sake
even though I walk
through the darkest valley
I fear no evil
for you are with me
your rod and your staff
they comfort me
You prepare a table before me
in the presence of my enemies
you anoint my head with oil
my cup overflows
surely goodness and mercy
will follow all the days of my
   life,

and I shall dwell
   in the House of the Lord

my whole life long.

we recite on the church video
I long to go outside.
our legs in old army blankets,
pale lambs embrace, a comfort
in bread, in wine, holy meals
this empty trail, now alone I
bleach clothes, count masks,
pacing every afternoon
past the old farm, neighbor,
only selfishness, for company,
viral exhale, invisible particles
in the hospital sterile,
miles before we rest,
sleeplessly checking news
what I took for granted, and
all this time dishsoap rainbow,
like sap from the running,
buckets you bury,
this death which must break
   us, eventually

mourning eternal your
   beardscratch kisses
side by side across the floral
   tablecloth

Thaw

Stop running—
the trail waits like an open door
snow filled hollow, sugar maple
sap like a river, ribbons of ice.
Pause on it trusting, it forgives everything
that kept you from this place
that made you speak and not listen
move and not stand still.

Stop running—
stack heartbeat on heartbeat
like a cairn fix direction,
hand raised like a mountain
maybe a spell, maybe a prayer.
Falcon, shadowing eager ground,
maybe a harrier, maybe a merlin,
so why not choose, everyday

to err on the side of magic,
believe bird and rock and endless sky
will speak miracles if you let them
unfurl as you exhale, take
your heart with them as they bound.
All stars and eastwind
companionate moving
universe speaking,

we are all already everything—
the salmon, the springdeer
the merlinfalcon, gyring.
Believe it, breath of their passing
already soft, already reborn
already at our destination
already safeback home.

From Here

It started when I crossed the river,
so much water
headfirst like a wildthing,
it felt like being born again, that breath.

Our first eveing, oldhouse waking
all the grayhaired ghosts came to whisper,
this is where the Christmas Tree goes,
this is how you knead the bread,

lost buttons, earrings, barbie shoes
appearing in the center of the rug,
as if I had just failed to look,
gardenbloom of strawberries overrun with bittersweet.

I turned a corner when our oven broke
upcounty repairman told me weeks,
meaning months, meaning,
when it was time, and not before,

slowheat rising like an answer,
macandcheese and brisket, castiron skillet
right on the coals, that magmic shimmer,
green with fragrant fire, summergold from flame.

Now our cabin, strong for winter,
hours knit and perled, grow long with sun.
Everything settles, finds true shape,
a rosary of cracks, these beads, these prayers.

In our backyard, a doe and her buck,
shoulder by shoulder, take calm shelter.
Good neighbors, we detour
past hoofprints and bittrunks

place seeds in the hemlockhollow
plant brackenfern, bramble,
jewelweed and winterberry,
clear every sharp stone our living made, away.

LandTrust Vishop Adam Postcard Russian Mud Instead A Troubling Before The first You Pitch Saturday Before Hot Kudzu We linger Persephone Tips The ivory If Gaw: What Persephone Trojan Prayer Burning Avalon ABC You One Nocture On Thanksgiving picture The ghost Things Trailblazer Tips The day We Socially The day My Golden Damariscotta Day Sestina Psalm Thaw From Here Earth and Go...

Earth and Spirit

Draw the Worldcard, eternal,
Light the sweetsage, thistle,
blood candle, purify every shadow,
blueviolet, purple.
Drive the circle,
you still know the way
in darkness, in blindness
find the outline
of your young dreams.

Reliquary, sanctuary
this pilgrimage, prostrate
at the feet of your past,
splinter tooth, fingernail
seeking some grasp
of bone on timebleached bone.
Former address, blank,
the raw field where once
our houses stood.

Come seeking resolution
compassion,
Open the doorsign,
Pour the redwine,
String the bead, a newmoon mala,
transit summer stars, our palms,
oracles, signs and wonders
on streetcorners, magnolia
leaves evergreen.

From the rust iron you have made a garden.
From chainmail, a jewel.
Hungry, now, our lostfeast comes
books still waiting exactly where we put them
on the windowsill, by the sunflowers,
spiralgalaxies forming
inhale, the breath we take,
what refuses eclipse,
what will never change.

Gratitude

There are endless people who call a book into being— giving deepest thanks is the very best part.

to Lis McLoughlin and NatureCulture, thank you for seeing the spirit of this collection and guiding it so gently and perfectly into being. It has been a privilege.

to Martin Bridge for the generous access to *Seven Tines*, the image that inspires and informs this book.

to Samaa Abdurraqib for expert insight and cherished guidance in the forming of this book.

to CMarie Fuhrman, Robert Carr, and Claire Millikin, for their generous and eloquent blurbs.

to Agnes and Jim Bushell, Nearshore and Porch poets, and all the women balancing, always.

to Gary Lawless, for steadfast support and constant inspiration.

to Gregory and Elizabeth Hagopian for finishing touches.

and finally, for my family: Betty and Greg, Judy and Les, my foundation. Sophia and Adam, you make everything and everywhere home. And, finally, my beloved and ever-supportive husband, Chris.

www.ingramcontent.com/pod-product-compliance
Lightning Source LLC
Chambersburg PA
CBHW051037030426
42336CB00015B/2927